THE MIND'S TOOLBOX

A Guide to "fixing your broken mind"

Bonnie Bawiec

Edited by: Matt Deuerlein

Introduction

When your leg is broken, what do you do?

Consult with a doctor, get a cast, maybe

medication & even physical therapy?

If I broke my leg and told you

I was going to take a chain saw and

cut it off because I cannot walk,

you would tell me that is too extreme,

that my leg is fixable,

that it might take time,

but it will heal.

Do not make a permanent decision

because of a temporary problem, right?

Well, that is the same approach

you should take with your mind.

If you are having trouble mentally,

I am here to tell you, its temporary

its fixable,

it may take time,

but you can think and feel better again.

This workbook is intended to work alongside your current mental health plan. It is for self-reflection on changing your perspective and giving you the skills necessary to think through depression. You can take control and play an active role in your recovery if you have the right tools. As with anything new, you must practice consistently in order to form a new habit.

*I believe that the key to success in learning something new is to be able to relate it to something you already know. Example: If I handed you a plate of food, and told you to eat it, and you didn't recognize it, what might you ask me? What is it? What does it taste like? We want to relate it to something we have already tasted. This is the same with anything unknown, any change. What is it **like?** Throughout this workbook, I will use examples to better understand these concepts.*

As a crisis clinician and certified life coach, I began creating group therapy worksheets that would focus on the future rather than dwell on the past. The following topics are based off of group therapy sessions that have been found highly successful and something that can be done independently, or with your therapist.

Extras: Driving Lessons, how to cope through an anxiety attack, goal setting, relationship 101, and 10 steps to living life without regret.

Day one: **Understanding the importance of your thoughts.**
This is the first step to starting recovery. If you think nothing
will work, you are setting yourself up for failure.

Day two: **Giving your past a purpose and a place.** This
chapter is crucial to be able to keep moving forward with your
life. When we focus too much on the past, we lose sight of
what is ahead and crash.

Day three: **Finding your purpose and learning to be selfish.**
This is a two-part section because they go hand in hand. If you
aren't selfish, you won't live according to your purpose. If you
don't have a purpose, you'll always put everyone else before
yourself. Both these behaviors are self-destructive because
you must take care of yourself first.

Day four: **Identifying and implementing coping skills.** You
need tools and you need to know when to use them. This
exercise will teach you to explore what works for you and
what your plan is.

Day five: **What it really means to be positive.** This is clarifying
the difference in being happy versus positive. While you can
maintain a positive outlook during a stressful time, it doesn't
mean you are any less frustrated.

Day six: **How to handle overwhelming situations.** This is a
more detailed look into the cognitive coping skills mentioned
in day four.

Day seven: **How to schedule happiness.** We get so caught up
on autopilot that we forget to slow down and add happiness
to our routine. You can enjoy moments during chaos.

Day 1

I firmly believe in the self-fulfilling prophecy. By definition, the self-fulfilling prophecy is a prediction that causes itself to be true. If you believe you can be successful, your actions will reflect your beliefs.

For example, *if I say that there are no good jobs around here, I cannot find any jobs, there aren't any places hiring, my mindset will block the available options out there. If I think to myself that I will find a job, and search for the one that fits my criteria, I will find options.*

Many people complain of racing and/or ruminating thoughts. They claim they can't help it. Let me tell you a secret - you can!

Think about this, close your eyes and imagine an...apple tree. Big brown trunk, green leafy bushes, red apples scattered throughout. Now think of a childhood memory that you love. Finally, visualize an orange and black butterfly fluttering around.

Open your eyes. See what you did? You controlled and changed your thoughts.

Inside your brain you are constantly sending and receiving messages. Imagine your mind is like a mailroom...tiny workers sorting through the messages and sending them throughout your mind and body. All day long your mind is telling your body what to do, feel, and think. At any moment, you (the boss) can come on over the loud speaker and say, "listen to me! Watch this!" When you closed your eyes and imagined an apple tree, you stopped all the tiny workers in your brain. You have control of your thoughts at any time, but you have to believe that you do. You have to think, "I don't like these thoughts. I am going to think about *(fill in the blank)* instead.

Next time you find yourself ruminating or having racing thoughts, try this approach.

Think of a counter thought. Think of something you like, something you enjoy doing, or possible outcomes both good and bad for problem situation.

Take control. It is empowering!

So how do you do this?

What is something that you find yourself ruminating about? *(The term comes from a cow, chewing over and over what has already been chewed and swallowed.)*

_____

_____

_____

_____

_____

_____

_____

_____

_____

What triggers your racing thoughts?

This is a stressor or a problem that initially looks impossible, is difficult, or time consuming.

_____

_____

_____

_____

_____

_____

_____

_____

_____

_____

_____

What steps can you take to change these thoughts when they come to mind?

_____

_____

_____

_____

_____

_____

_____

_____

_____

_____

Remember, doing something new is like tying your shoes. When you first learned, you were clumsy, you messed up, and you got frustrated. But now, you do it automatically without thinking. Learning to think requires repetitive action. You must do it again and again, even when you are frustrated, even when you mess up. The more you do it, the easier it gets.

Day 2

Imagine you have a shoebox full of pictures from your past. You look at them from time to time, remembering the memory. They are good memories, happy experiences that you cherish. But you do not carry them around and show them to everyone you meet. That kindergarten picture is wonderful, but it's not necessary to relive that picture every day. It is fun to look at sometimes, though.

Just like positive memories, negative memories are visual experiences in your mind. You hold onto them and replay them over and over again. This is normal, and it is okay to look at it from time to time the way you reflect on your box of photographs, but it is not necessary to carry them with you wherever you go. They do not need to be included with every interaction. There are times when reflecting on a past hurtful experience is helpful in guiding us with the current situation. Just don't replay it all day every day.

Here are the key points to giving your past a purpose and a place:

- *Accept that the past has happened.* There is no time machine to go back and change it. You have no other choice!
- *What can you learn from the past? What have you gained?* Even negative situations contribute to you. Example: Frequent moving = gained ability to adapt to new environments, meet new people, learn new areas etc. Example: relationship break-up = learn characteristics that you don't want in a companion, ability to assert yourself and say no, identifying wants and needs, chance to find companion more compatible, etc.
- *Allowing time to reflect on past, not dwell on past.* It is important and necessary to remember your past. *Blocking* is destructive and a form of self-sabotage. When you use all your energy to avoid thinking about the past, you end up making the emotion tied to that memory larger. If the memory is something painful, that hurt will be greater when it comes up. The past cannot be avoided. *Dwelling* is also a form of self-sabotage. Dwelling prevents moving forward because you are too focused on what has already happened; your vision of the present and future are blocked.

- *Learning how to reflect appropriately on past.* Our minds bring back past memories from time to time. It is important to think through the event/emotion and link it to your present now. Is this something that is similar to now? Do you need to relate a strength/coping skill that you used then that you can use now? Are you going through a hardship now that you need to remember and encourage yourself that you are capable of handling? Is this something recurrent that you need to revisit to find a solution to fix?

- *Understanding the difference between flashbacks/panic attacks and memories.* A flashback is often a sensational memory of the past. It can be visual, auditory, taste, smell, or physical. It often elicits a physical response, such as shaking, sweating, fast breathing, or muscle tightening. A panic attack could occur with a flashback or on its own. A panic attack is when your mind says fear, and your body responds. Panic attack symptoms may vary. What are your symptoms? Understanding how to cope with flashbacks/panic attacks are crucial to minimizing their frequency and eventually having those past events as simply a memory. Learning the triggers/symptoms of a panic attack can lessen the intensity by shortening the length of time in panic mode.

- *Focusing perspective on present and future.* Make a to-do list of your wants and needs. Create goals to make your future better than your past. Surround yourself with support and positivity. Know your limits and back away when it becomes "too much." Reflect on your wants/needs and situation often so that you can keep moving forward.

Once you can accept your past as part of you, whether it is good or bad, you can be "free" of the chain holding you back. You can release yourself to freely continue on your journey.

Holding onto your past is like staring at your rearview mirror. Look too long and you crash off the road. Simply look every now and then, and then refocus back on what's ahead.

So how do you do this?

How has the past contributed to who you are as a person? What strengths have you gained?

_____
_____
_____
_____
_____
_____
_____

What triggers and symptoms do you experience during a flashback/panic attack?

_____
_____
_____
_____
_____
_____
_____

Is this past experience something that needs to be revisited? Is it guidance for your current situation?

_____
_____

_____

_____

_____

_____

_____

What coping skills can be utilized? How can you reflect on past in a positive way? *(Note: this does not mean it was a HAPPY memory; to look at something positive, you are looking for the good that could come out of it)*

_____

_____

_____

_____

_____

_____

What are your wants and needs in life?

_____

_____

_____

_____

_____

_____

Day 3

Why are you alive right now? If you could do anything you wanted tomorrow, next week, or next year, what would it be? Now spin it around, if you died tomorrow, would you be able to smile at what you did today? Would you be satisfied that you did the best you could?

Let's back up. You are breathing. You are alive. You have the opportunity to live. Pick - what do you want your life to be?

I have one question to ask you: "Why not?"

Fill in the blank. Life is_____.

Life is all about making memories, sharing moments, experiencing the journey with those you love, doing good, celebrating....right? Life HAS obstacles, trauma, heartaches, frustration. Life can be unfair but at the end of the day, life is an opportunity. Every day.

You cannot always change the circumstances that you face, but you can choose how you handle them.

It is a shame that society has made the word "selfish" a bad word. Let me explain.

Who do you spend the most time with? Who is one person that you know every memory, every thought, and emotion? Who do you have no choice but to be around 24/7? <u>YOURSELF.</u> So if you do not advocate for yourself, if you don't communicate your wants and needs, who is? If you do not work on your life and your journey, who is? If you hate yourself and the circumstances you're in, then how do you think you will stay focused on your purpose? Use the frustration and disappointment as fuel for a better tomorrow.

At the end of the day, you have you. So you have to be selfish. You have to care for yourself, accept your flaws and love who you are. If you have made mistakes, stop judging, learn and continue on. Take care of yourself first, and then with the left over energy, give to others. Example: you have a breakfast platter of eggs, bacon, sausage, toast, and fruit. You have two options – eat first and share what you have leftover, or offer everything away and eat what's left? Of course the correct answer is to eat first. You need to fuel your body. It's important for you to function. If you only ate what's left, you would feel deprived and sluggish.

Feed yourself first. Be selfish, it's a necessity. Only give your "extra."

So how do you do this?

What is the purpose of your life?

_____
_____
_____
_____
_____
_____
_____

What do you want to do in your life?

_____
_____
_____
_____

What are you unhappy with right now?
What is your reasoning that you haven't changed
it? How can you change it? *If it is something out of
your control, how do you adjust to it?*

_____
_____
_____

Create a goal.

_____

What steps do you need to take to achieve this goal?

_____

_____

_____

_____

_____

_____

_____

When do you want to accomplish this goal?

_____

How will you handle the obstacles/setbacks that get in the way?

_____

_____

_____

_____

Day 4

Coping skills are necessary to help you handle difficult situations or emotions. It is important to have more than one coping skill due to varying situations. No matter what, the best practice is to have a <u>PLAN.</u>

> *Think about it this way – imagine you have a toolbox filled with various tools. If your toilet is clogged, what do you do? You reach for the plunger because it is the right tool. Now imagine you have a picture that needs to be hung on the wall, and you tried using the same plunger as your tool. Should you throw out the plunger and quit because it isn't working? No.*
> *Re-evaluate the situation. Can you use another tool? The plunger is a great tool, but not the right tool for that specific task.*

Understanding which coping skills to use and when is key to your success.

Types of Coping Skills

- ✓ *Diversion/Distraction*
  - o These coping skills are for temporary relief. They are meant to *distract* or *divert* your attention away from the racing thoughts.
  - o You may use one of these coping skills after getting into an argument with someone, or you're worried about an event of the near future.
  - o A few examples of these coping skills include: writing, painting, gardening, going for a walk, watching TV, listening to music, playing a game/cards, going shopping, or reading.
  - o Unfortunately, many people ONLY have diversion/distraction coping skills. These do *NOT* help with chronic or recurring stressors.
- ✓ *Social*
  - o These coping skills help you handle your relationships with other people.
  - o You might use a *social* coping skill when facing a strained relationship

or if there is tension that is difficult to communicate.

- These *communication/social* skills might include: talking to someone you trust that is unbiased to the situation, setting boundaries, identifying your limits, learning when to say "no", writing a letter to the person (doesn't mean you have to give it-sometimes it helps to "get it off your chest"), using humor, setting aside time to get together, or helping someone in need (person or pet).

✓ *Cognitive (thinking)*

- This set of coping skills can make or break us. We must be able to *THINK* through a situation and have the right perspective.
- Another way to remember this type of coping skill is to think of it as problem solving. Ask yourself HOW do I fix this?
- Examples of ways to utilize this coping skill are: brainstorming possible solutions to fix issue,

writing a pro and con list, reviewing your expectations of the situation, using empathy, writing out a to-do list, reading inspirational quotes to help empower a positive attitude, practicing flexibility to change, making a gratitude list, or taking a "mental health" day to pamper yourself by doing something you enjoy.

✓ *Tension Releasers/Physical*
- o If you currently have a *negative or harmful* coping skill such as cutting, burning, punching, destruction, then it is helpful to replace that self-mutilation or aggression with a *physical* coping skill.
- o Our muscles respond to stress. *Tension releasing* coping skills help release pressure in our body physically to help us relax.
- o Examples of these coping skills are exercising, taking a hot/cold shower, squeezing a stress ball, crying, laughing, playing with play-doh/clay, ripping up paper, progressive muscle relaxation, deep breathing, rubbing

ice cubes on your skin, drinking hot tea/cocoa, getting a good night's sleep, eating a well-balanced diet, limiting caffeine, or meditation.

Tips for success:

- ✓ Talk to someone you trust
- ✓ Follow your treatment plan for your medication and therapy
- ✓ Write down your frustrations and make a list of what you can do to feel better
- ✓ Set aside time to be alone and reflect
- ✓ Overcome negative self-talk. Strengthen your self-esteem.
- ✓ Reduce your load. Set limits. Be assertive.
- ✓ Consider the big picture. Temporary vs. Permanent
- ✓ Accept the past. You cannot change it!
- ✓ Communicate your wants and needs. You are your best advocate!
- ✓ Set goals. Make a to-do list.
- ✓ Focus on the positive.
- ✓ Fuel your energy for each day.

So how do you do this?

To create a plan, first think about the problems that cause you stress.

_____

_____

Do you have control over it/can you change it?   Yes or No

If yes, what steps can you take to change it? Who can you reach out to for help?

_____

_____

_____

_____

_____

_____

_____

If no, how can you cope with those negative feelings? What impact will it have on your life? How can you adjust your routine or surroundings to handle this stress? What can you do?

_____

_____

_____

_____

_____

_____

_____

What kind of coping skills work for you? Do you have at least one per type? *(Distraction, Social, Cognitive, and Physical)*

_____

_____

_____

_____

_____

_____

_____

Day 5

What does it really mean to be positive? Does this mean you should be happy all the time? Does this mean that there aren't any problems? No. Having a positive approach means that you process through the bad situations using a combination of realism and optimism. Not everything is going to work out as you would like or as planned; however, accepting that and looking for an alternative that is comparable is the correct approach.

Accept your past trauma. Whatever it was, you're still standing. You fought, and you survived. You made it through the time that you looked at as "the worst." This is a strength, so feel empowered. This is a motivator for whatever stress you are facing now. You can overcome this obstacle.

Find the benefit. Balance your reasoning and emotion. There is a lesson to be learned from each negative experience. There is also a gain with every loss. Example: if you got a flat tire and were stuck on the side of the road, you may find yourself stressed. You may be late for wherever you were going, or maybe you don't have money in the budget for this right now. The positive is that it can be fixed. You have a spare in the trunk — you might be late, but you will get there. The situation is temporary and fixable. Thinking this way doesn't make you excited that you have a flat, but it makes it manageable, and it doesn't consume you.

So how do you do this?

If I know the answer to "why," will it change my life?

_____

_____

_____

_____

Can the situation be changed? Is it temporary?

_____

_____

_____

_____

What can I do right now to make this difficult time easier?

_____

_____

_____

_____

How are you a survivor? How can you keep fighting?

_____

_____

_____

_____

What is one situation you can view positively?

_____

_____

_____

_____

_____

_____

_____

_____

_____

_____

_____

Day 6

We find ourselves in stressful situations often. How can we be more productive with our stress?

Think about this – we get frustrated often. What is good about frustration? Frustration is the fuel for change! When we are frustrated, we evaluate our current situation and look for what we can do better.

A lot of energy is used that lead us to dead ends. In the examples below, the same energy is used but is refocused.

What is something changeable? No income. What is something unchangeable? Death of a loved one.

Illustration A.

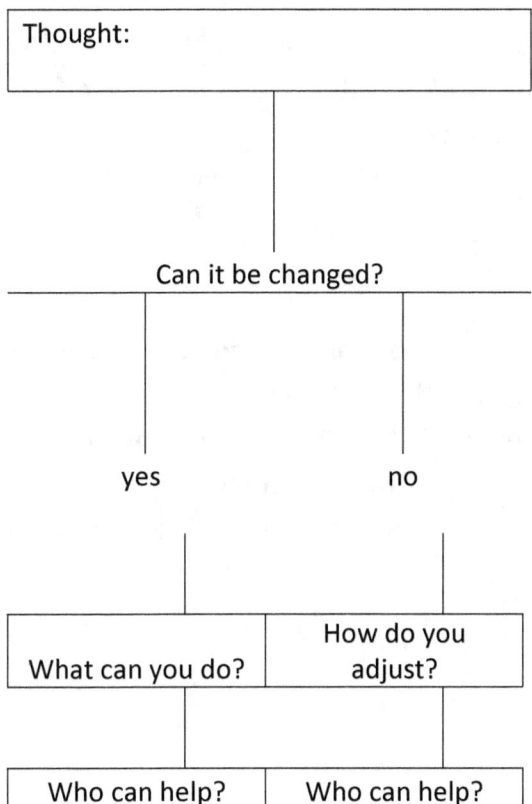

Example: Need income.

What can I do? – Apply for jobs, apply for disability, miscellaneous work, sell items, or donate blood are just a few examples

Example: Death of a loved one.

How do I cope? – What part of them is a part of me (mannerisms, traditions)? What can I do to celebrate them? What can I do that I enjoyed doing with them in remembrance of them? How can I fill my schedule now that my time won't be spent with them?

Tips for success!

- *Come up with a motto to repeat in certain stressful situations. Example: Not my circus, not my monkeys, or to each its own, or it is what it is etc.*
- *Make your plan viewable. Put it on paper.*
- *Pick a time to think about your stress. Remind yourself to stick to it. Don't spend all day on it.*
- *Try to avoid "blocked thinking." If you look at all the ways it can go wrong, you will worry yourself sick. Be proactive and look for what can go right, while minimizing catastrophe.*

So how do you do this?

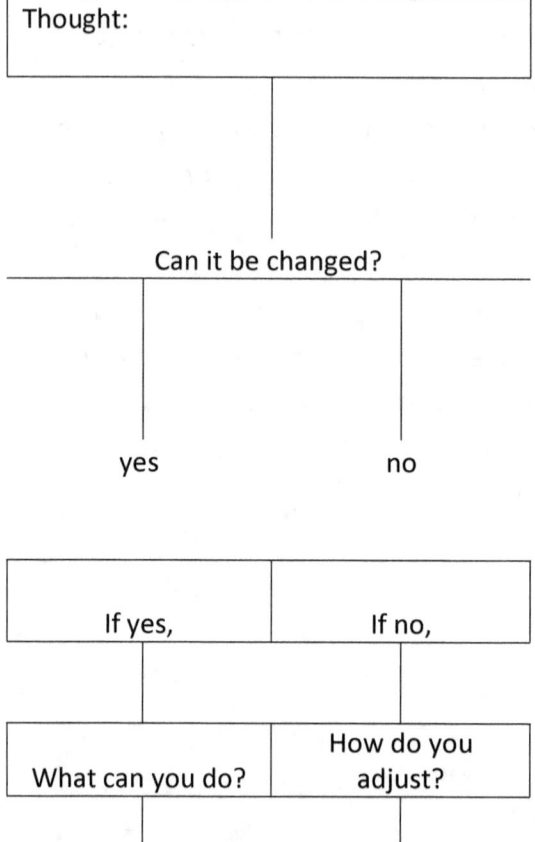

Thought:

Can it be changed?

yes   no

If yes,   If no,

What can you do?   How do you adjust?

Who can help?   Who can help?

What is the stress? Can you change it? How do you adjust?

_____

_____

_____

_____

_____

_____

_____

_____

_____

_____

_____

_____

_____

_____

_____

_____

_____

Create a to-do list. Number them in order of priority.

_____

_____

_____

_____

_____

_____

_____

How can you stick to your list?

_____

_____

Day 7

Why is it important to have happiness?

There is no guarantee for your life. You have right now, why reserve its worth for a maybe? Take that adventure you've always wanted. Make a plan to make things happen now. Don't put off what you wish for, start working on getting it.

What is something you want to do in the next month?

_____

_____

In the next 6 months?

_____

_____

In the next year?

_____

_____

Next 5 years?

_____

_____

We get so caught up on auto-pilot that we forget to slow down and enjoy the little moments, or take time for ourselves. Think about this – if someone passed away and you got a phone call about the funeral, you would drop your plans and go say good-bye? Why don't we drop our plans for celebrations? Stop putting happiness off! Enjoy your life, take opportunities – this is your chance, big or small.

What is your typical routine?

_____

_____

Add one thing that is fun/that makes you happy

_____

_____

What is your "me" time? If you cannot have it daily, how can you add it weekly?

_____

_____

Check in!

How do you feel? Easier said than done? Of course. As with anything new, it's uncomfortable at first. It feels awkward and it takes conscious thought. But with consistent practice daily, you can create a new habit of healthy thinking!

Remember, you are in control. You have the power to steer your mind and your life whichever way you choose. Surround yourself with motivation and support. Look for new things to do. Stick with the people who encourage you to be the best you.

Congratulations! You are making progress, even if you don't see it yet. You have made it through each day of this workbook because you want to be better. No matter how exhausted you are, or how many times you feel you failed, here you are.

*The following pages are "extras" to help with your success. Repeat these over and over if needed. Make it a habit. Your mental health is like taking a bath. You can't work on it once and think you never have to do it again. No, you need to bathe daily because life happens and you get dirty. You need to work on your mental health daily, because life happens. ☺BB.

Driving Lessons

In order to Drive *(plan)* successfully, you need to understand how your car *(life)* works.

If you want to go forward, you need to be in DRIVE. Drive *(your goal/plan)* means having a destination to go to, and actively working towards it. Drive is taking steps towards what you want.

While driving, it is okay, and necessary, to glance in the rearview and side view mirrors *(your past).* It is dangerous for you *(your mind)* and car *(your life and those in it)* to focus on what is behind you in those mirrors because you will be unable to keep the car on the road. If you stare too long *(dwell),* you will crash. You cannot keep looking behind and expect to stay on track.

It is okay to remember your past, remember where it brought you, and keep going.

You cannot drive somewhere new if you don't know how to get there. You need a map (plan).

When you're driving to your destination (goal) you are excited (motivated), it might be long, and you might get tired, but you don't quit, you don't turn back. You remind yourself of that destination and think of how far you've come and how you cannot wait to get there.

For example: you are taking a vacation to the beach. The beach is 5 hours away. You are excited. Driving for long periods of time can take a toll on you – your legs start getting sore, you have to use the bathroom, you get hungry. You'll likely need to stop and take a break. Do you pull into the rest stop and think, "this is taking too long. I am just going to quit. I am not driving anymore!", or do you think, "I can't wait to get there! The beach is going to be so nice! I can't believe I drove over 100 miles so far, only 300 more to go!"

That's how you should view your goal. Your goal is something you want that will make you better. You remind yourself of how much happier or better off your life will be when you achieve your goal and you keep pushing towards it!

The time will pass anyway, so do it! Get in your car and go!

How to cope through an anxiety attack

1. I am safe.
2. These feelings will fade.
3. This can't hurt me.
4. I can get air. I can take a deep breath. (smell the flowers, blow out the candles)
5. I am starting to relax.
6. I feel calmer.
7. I am going to be okay.
8. What can I do that will make me happy?
9. Who can I talk to?
10. Count from 10-1 slowly.

Tips:

Can you leave the room, and walk slowly focusing on each step you take.

Look around you. What do you see?

What were you just doing before the attack?

Can you do something else?

Imagine there is a TV screen inside your mind. What image can you put on the screen that is something positive/something you like/something relaxing? Close your eyes. Try to visualize the image on the screen.

What are the lyrics to your favorite song?

Goal Setting

What do you want?

_____

_____

_____

_____

What are the steps you need to take to get it?

1. _____

_____

2. _____

_____

3. _____

_____

4. _____

_____

How can you achieve these steps?

_____

_____

_____

_____

What timeline do you want to be able to complete these goals?

_____

_____

_____

_____

What obstacles might get in the way or slow you down?

_____

_____

_____

_____

How can you overcome these obstacles?

_____

_____

_____

_____

What will you gain by achieving those goals?

_____

_____

_____

_____

Relationships

We have expectations for every person we encounter. We don't necessarily voice our expectations for their role. For example, when you check out at the grocery store, you don't explain the steps you expect the cashier to do (please ring up each item, ask for my savings card, bag my groceries, and accept my payment).

Apply this to EVERYONE in your life.

Think about friendships, your spouse, and your family members. You have expectations of them but you don't typically voice them.

What is your ideal _____ role?
(friend, family, etc)

_____

_____

_____

_____

What is your ideal spouse?

_____

_____

_____

_____

Conflicts occur because they aren't meeting your expectation, or you are not meeting theirs.

Communication is important. Speak up-not by name-calling/blaming/putting the other person down, but by expressing your wants and needs to them and give them direction of what you would like (what is wrong, and what is the plan from here).

Understand and respect the other person may differ from your expectation and that's okay!

Break-ups are good! Yes it is painful, but it's better to find someone you are more compatible with. Break-ups give you perspective – you learn characteristics that you don't want in a companion, gain the ability to assert self and say no, identify your wants and needs, and have the chance to find someone better suited for you.

Living your life with no regrets

1. Have purpose.
   a. What do you want your life to be?
2. Don't waste time.
   a. Stop putting off your to-do list.
   b. Stop saying "I will do this when…"
3. You are not a victim.
   a. You are a survivor, a fighter.
   b. You have overcome obstacles in the past; you can continue to overcome any present or future problems.
4. Every day is a new beginning.
   a. Just because you have had a bad life, doesn't mean you need to have a bad future.
   b. Just because you make a mistake, doesn't mean you can't correct it and move forward.
5. Stop making excuses.
   a. Don't compare yourself to others.
   b. Don't think of what you can't do; focus on what you can do.
6. Let go of self-sabotage.
   a. Meaning: when you prepare for something but find every reason not

to do it, you are stopping yourself from achieving it.

7. Give up the "what if."
   a. What if it doesn't work? No, what if it does!?

8. Step outside your comfort zone.
   a. Change doesn't happen when you continue to do the same thing.
   b. If you want something different, you must do something different.

9. Ask for help.
   a. You are not the master of everything.
   b. It is a strength to ask for help.
   c. You can learn something new every day.
   d. Find a mentor to motivate you and inspire you.

10. Don't give up!
    a. Perfection is never the goal. Strive for progress.
    b. Every day, every step, keep moving forward!